Nico De Swert

LIVING WITH FLOWERS

Nico De Swert
LIVING WITH FLOWERS

PHOTOGRAPHY BY WENDELL T. WEBBER

TEXT BY KATHLEEN HACKETT

ABRAMS, NEW YORK

CONTENTS

PREFACE

Many years ago my mother took me to a demonstration put on by floral designers in Antwerp, Belgium, where I grew up. I was amazed at how skillful they were and how technical and sculptural their designs. That day it dawned on me that floral design could be my calling. I soon discovered that becoming a fine floral artist requires constant study—of nature, color, and textures. What began as a general appreciation and passing interest evolved into my art and my passion—making sculpture from what nature provides.

Why flowers? Flowers are alive, they change from moment to moment, and they tell a story. What's more, my manner of working with blossoms, stems, leaves, and grasses is not unlike shaping a character for the stage. Floral design is much more than filling vases and containers. It is the study of a flower's personality through it's color, size, stance, and texture. Because plant materials possess a great diversity of textures, the opportunities to cast them in unusual ways are almost endless. For example, mattress fern can be woven into a sort of tapestry (page 73) from which flowers can be hung. All plant materials have a natural drama that I try to translate into sculptural pieces that speak volumes. In fact, long before spoken languages developed, flowers were considered "information carriers," their shapes and shades the components of a pictorial language.

My style is heavily influenced by Belgian, Dutch, and German artists. For some reason it is flowers rather than paint or clay or fabric that compel me to create a mood or express a sentiment. Flower arranging is like fashion now—every season there's a new trend, a new color; it's constantly evolving, and the options are endless, so it's fresh and exciting all the time. But I believe I am more of a floral sculptor than arranger. Rather than recreate nature in a vase, I am much more inclined to recast it. After all, how can one outdo Mother Nature? I could never compete with her, but I can make something new. Once you remove flowers from their natural habitats, however, an immediate battle with nature begins. The process of dying is set in motion and you must work quickly because picked flowers change rapidly. This forces one to appreciate the vitality of life and the delicacy of decay. I love equally a flower before it blooms and one that is curling toward death. The unconventionally beautiful, such as tulips just past its peak, are sometimes more preferable than traditional—and too often expected—blooms.

Color, however, is my primary inspiration, and the floral designs presented here are organized by color to reflect that. I prefer shades of the same color rather than a riotous combination of hues; it allows me to create cleaner lines, defined shapes, and decidedly sculptural pieces. By using layered tones of the same color, you can play with scale, varying textures, and proportion without confusing the eye. Whatever the color and combination of flowers, they will usually tell you what they want to be. All too often, I set out with a specific design in mind that inevitably changes as I begin to work with the flowers. The key is to let the plant material inspire you as you go.

I always begin my work with the container and often I'll do a sketch of the concept beforehand. For me the shape of the container dictates the shape of the arrangement. Once you realize how true this is, you will never look at vases the same way again. I am obsessed with shapes and see possibilities in just about anything with sides and a bottom. For example, I used an oversized bottle cap that had been designed for an old Coca-Cola advertisement (page 16). Occasionally, if I can't find a vessel in the shape I am looking for, I'll make it: I created a "vase" out of pussy willows (page 63), and I used lemon leaves to form a container of sorts for the rose spheres on pages 40–41.

As a boy in Antwerp, I dreamed of spending my days on a stage, or at least in film, and had visions of Hollywood parading through my head. It wasn't until I was in the eighth grade that my parents sent me to weekly classes at the local art academy. I so clearly remember clutching my wooden briefcase-sized paint box under my arm every Wednesday and Saturday, while other boys headed off to scouts or soccer. Despite my love for painting and drawing, however, my well-meaning mother and father believed that technical school would set me on a certain path to success, and so for four years I struggled to stay engaged in math and sciences. When they finally realized that such left-brain subjects sapped my enthusiasm, they relented and sent me back to art school. Like many artists, I graduated still unsure of my medium. I liked painting and drawing, but they never felt entirely right for me. This was about the time when I attended the floral arranging demonstration where top Belgian and Dutch designers created wildly different arrangements from the same bunch of flowers. After that I began to work for my mother, who had just opened a flower

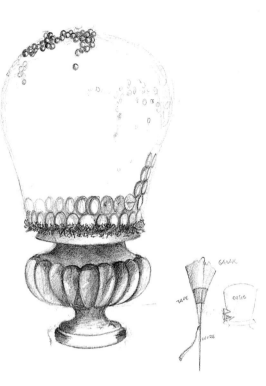

Design sketch for arrangement on page 130.

shop. At about the same time, my brother became the manager of the largest wholesale flower business in Europe. I eventually went to work for him, spending my days in the refrigerators where the flowers were organized by color and size after they came off the trucks. Then the owner of the company asked me to make a bouquet for a party he was attending later that evening. Needless to say, I was so nervous I could barely construct the arrangement, but I chose terra-cotta roses, orange ranunculus, and lemon leaves, and tied the bunch with unsure hands. Pleased with my work, the owner suggested I try merchandising and displaying for the Christmas and Easter flower markets, the largest and most important in the flower business. It was intimidating because my job was to inspire some of the most powerful flower companies in the world to buy flowers, but what I did not find daunting was the sheer variety of flowers at my fingertips. I could create whatever floral designs I wanted, with whatever flowers I wanted.

By sheer luck, one of my clients, who knew of my desire to move to the United States, invited me to come to New York City. With little more than my portfolio, I arrived determined to find myself a floral design job with one of the famous talents I had read about. I walked into every flower shop and showed my book to the top event and party planners in Manhattan. In three months' time I was working for Renny Reynolds. I also began to style flowers for magazines on the side, which led to a full-time position at *Martha Stewart Living* where my two passions, acting and floral design, miraculously came together.

The arrangements on the following pages are meant to inspire you to think about flowers and floral design in their infinite possibilities. I want to help you expand your ideas about flowers to encompass more than something you buy only on special occasions. In Europe, flowers are as much a part of daily life as coffee. Every town, no matter how small, has a florist, often more than one. It's this mentality that prompted the designers of the Volkswagen Beetle to install a tiny glass vase next to the steering wheel. I want to instill that same approach in this country, to encourage you to surround yourself with flowers—or branches, berries, leaves, greenery—in some way every day. It doesn't have to be complicated—a single flower in any kind of container will do. Gradually, I hope, you too will begin to see the theater they can create in your own home.

Nico De Swert

Narcissus
Salix.

Design sketch for page 63.

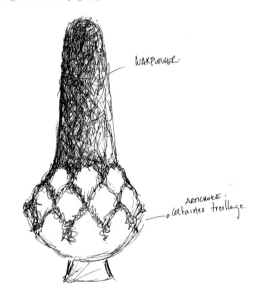

WAXFLOWER

ARTICHOKE
container treillage.

Design sketch for page 82.

GREEN

  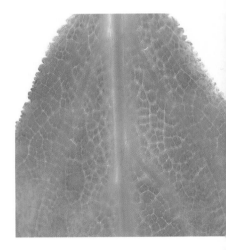

Green is symbolic of new beginnings. To be green is a gift, often appreciated only in hindsight. Who wouldn't relish a chance to return to the innocence of youth, to be bright with endless possibilities again? Green is among the most exciting—and promising—colors in nature. Stems, leaves, moss, berries, buds, twigs, grass, fruit, and flowers—whether newly opened or slightly wilted—offer an endlessly versatile palette for soothing, restive floral designs. The foliage of a crowd of hyacinth bulbs is as appealing as the flowers that eventually sprout from them. Immature dogwood branches, nimble in their greenness, can be bent and twisted into a clever cage for paper-thin ranunculus blossoms. One of nature's most surprising bequests, and perhaps its greatest reward, is its green blossoms.

RED

So besotted with Marc Anthony was Cleopatra that she served him a romantic meal in a room knee-deep in red roses. Colorful writer and raconteur Dorothy Parker used nine different shades of it in her living room. Whether called upon to incite passion or express it, red—or cranberry, claret, scarlet, vermilion, or Mandarin—instantly captures the eye and demands a response. Hummingbirds are drawn to the brightest flowers, especially red ones. Imagine the frenzy they would make around a bowl full of Sensational Fantasy or gloriosa! Red loves green, its complement—put them together, as in the Red-Berlin-and-lemon-leaf spheres (opposite page) and their intensity is heightened, not unlike the Egyptian queen and her Roman lover.

YELLOW

Claude Monet bathed the walls of his Giverny kitchen with it. Van Gogh applied it

thick as icing on his canvas to paint his famous sunflowers. What is it about a

sunny yellow room or a bunch of golden blooms that lightens the spirit? Of all

the colors in the spectrum, yellow is often described as the friendliest, the easiest

to like. Indeed, vibrant yellow narcissus are among the first flowers to greet us

each spring; they are harbingers of kindlier weather. And while a mix of sandy,

buttery, or golden flowers will impart light and luminosity to any room, they are

often overlooked when sleek and chic is required. Nevertheless, as the bold designs

and shapes on the following pages attest, yellow, too, can make the most powerful

statement in the room.

PINK

"Pink is the navy blue of India," style maven Diana Vreeland once declared.
Flowers, as in fashion, can defy color stereotypes. Pink petals and buds are
perhaps the most easily typecast, as they are often called upon to play to
our frilly, feminine side in arrangements that tend toward the treacly. But
when individual blossoms of fragrant pink pearl hyacinths are glued into
the shape of a perfect sphere and cradled in a vessel the same color as a
dark and stormy sky (page 75), the effect is more handsome, or perhaps
even alien-looking, than delicate. Pick apart a pretty pink rose and recon-
struct it—petal by petal, thorn by thorn—into a single rose called Illusion
(page 71) and nothing is more chic—or sentimental. It is a clever wink at
nature, one that would certainly have made Vreeland swoon.

PURPLE

As the sun sets below the horizon, a blue sky turns violet on its way to dusk, and for a brief moment in time, the world is a peaceful place. Did you ever notice how a lavender sky sheds a rarefied light on the earth beneath it? And when it casts its glow on blue flowers, the rarest blooms of all, the color is never richer or more intense. It is not surprising that purple flowers are among the most desireable of all. After all, it is the color that symbolizes what most of us seek—constancy and truth. When there's a vase of Sterling Silver roses to greet you in the hallway, or helleborus bursting at your bedside, you are sure to feel calmer, more ready to meet the day, whatever it may hold for you.

WHITE

It symbolizes peace, purity, and innocence. In some cultures, it is worn to funerals as an expression of hope. In all of its infinite shades—warm or cool, bright or muted —the color white has the power to utterly transform, yet, at the same time, remain subtle. Two clusters of eucharis (page 113) blooming out of jet-black containers are as eye-catching as any sculpture. A single white snowdrop, springing out of a silver vase (page 117), is simple and spare, but the impact is no less, much like a Basho haiku. Like the great Japanese poet's white chrysanthemum, only a closer look at the bloom reveals its faultless perfection.

BLACK

Its very existence is a result of the absence of light, yet its presence can be as uplifting as a sun-filled room. Though equated with night and death, black can be dramatic and elegant and dashing, more mod than morose. Consider the night sky, a Vermeer painting, a black-tie ball. And black flowers. Rare and remarkable in their dark grays, maroons, and violets, they possess a mysterious quality that immediately attracts attention. What could be more entrancing than the slightly curled edges of a single black anemone? Or more compelling than dozens of smoky-gray eucalyptus pods growing out of a white compote in the shape of an exotic hat (page 131)?

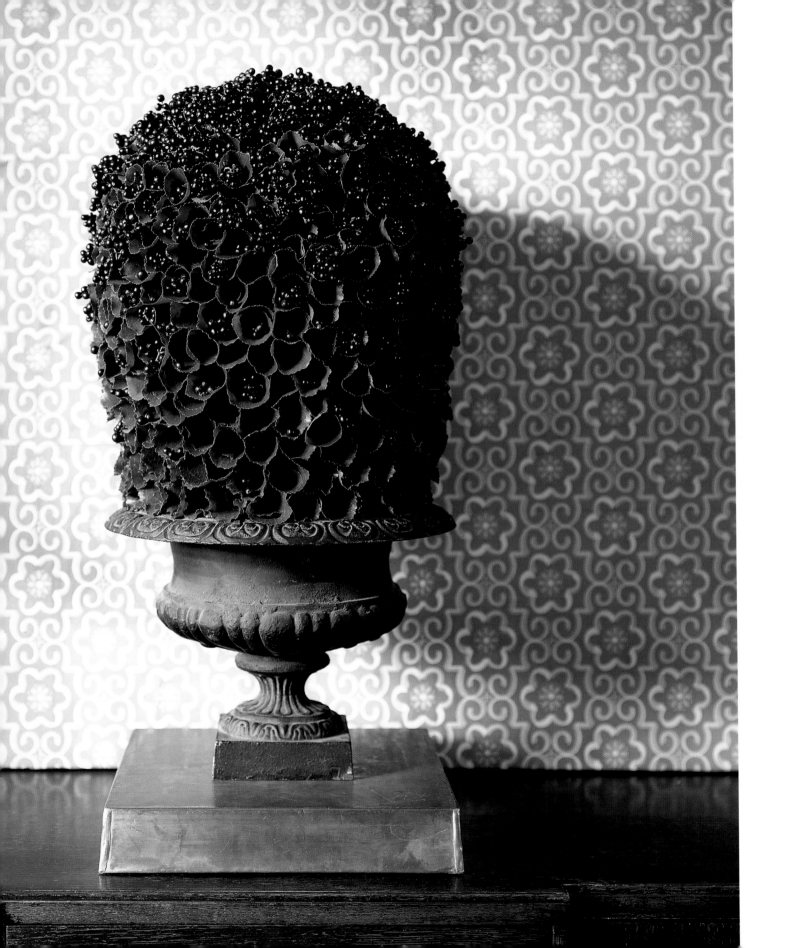

FLOWER CAPTIONS

PAGE 10 Shamrock chrysanthemum

PAGE 11 LEFT TO RIGHT Hypericum berries; Amaryllis; Lamb's ear

PAGE 12 Shamrock chrysanthemums

PAGE 13 Dates, mattress fern (container

PAGE 14 Anthurium, calla lilies, bear grass

PAGE 15 Anthurium, calla lily

PAGE 16 Carnations, bleached salix

PAGE 17 Ranunculus, moss, dogwood branches (the "cage")

PAGE 18 Ranunculus, snowballs, helleborus, cornus stems

PAGE 19 Ranunculus

PAGES 20–21 Ranunculus, amaryllis, paperwhites, silver alba leaves (glued onto the spheres as well as the "cuff" underneath the paperwhites)

PAGES 22–23 Chestnuts, viburnum berries, acorns

PAGE 24 Snowballs, roses (Illusion), magnolia branches and buds

PAGE 25 Snowballs

PAGES 26–27
Fritillaria, betula stems

PAGE 28
Hyacinth bulbs

PAGE 29
Hyacinth bulbs

PAGE 30 Asclepias

PAGE 31 Asclepias,
Dusty Miller, dates

PAGE 32 Pears,
pear leaves

PAGE 33 Setaria grass

PAGE 34 Roses (Red
Berlin), lemon leaves

PAGE 35 LEFT TO RIGHT
Ranunculus, cordeline
leaves; Anthurium;
Roses (Red Berlin)

PAGES 36–37
Ranunculus, cordeline
leaves

PAGES 38–39
Mattress fern (grassy
container), apples, crab
apples, bear grass

PAGES 40–41 Roses (Red
Berlin), lemon leaves

YELLOW

PAGES 58–59
Ranunculus

PAGES 60–61 Roses
(Mambo), magnolia leaves

PAGE 62 Roses
(Clementine), boxwood
leaves

PAGE 63 Narcissus,
pussy willows

PAGES 64–65
Ranunculus

PAGE 66 Rose (Aqua)

PAGE 67 LEFT TO RIGHT
Rose (Illusion); Gerber
daisy; Calla lily

PAGE 68 Roses (Sterling
Silver), magnolia leaves

PAGE 69 Roses (Diadeem
and Magenta Diadeem)

PAGE 70 Hydrangeas

PAGE 71 Rose (Illusion);
the container is made of
rose leaves, then thorns
glued onto the stem, and
additional petals were
glued on to expand the
blossom

PAGE 72 Cymbidium,
birch twigs

PAGE 73 Cymbidium,
mattress fern (hanging to
which flower containers
are attached), galax leaves

PAGES 90–91 Roses (Sterling Silver), Dusty Miller

PAGES 92–93 Anemones, grape hyacinth, bleached salix, goose eggshells

PAGES 94–95 Fritillaria

PAGES 96–97 Hyacinth blossoms, boxwood leaves

PAGE 98 Sweet peas, smilex leaves

PAGE 99 Hosta leaves (bottom), sweet peas (middle), agapanthus (top)

PAGE 100 Velvet flower

PAGE 101 LEFT TO RIGHT Anemone; Orchid; Clematis

PAGE 102 Calla lilies

PAGE 103 Anemones

PAGES 104–105 Clematis

PAGE 122 Lily of the valley

PAGE 123 Pitcher plants, clump moss

PAGE 124 Calla lilies

PAGE 125 LEFT TO RIGHT Calla lilies; Anemone; Fiddlehead ferns

PAGE 126 Chocolate cosmos, snake grass

PAGE 127 Anemone

PAGES 128–129 Roses (Red Berlin and Black Beauty), hydrangeas, sweet peas, irises, ranunculus, calla lilies, tulips (Parrot), artichokes, fiddlehead ferns

PAGE 130 Galax leaves, sambucus nigra

PAGE 131 Eucalyptus pods

FLOWER ARRANGING TIPS

All of the following tips are intended to extend the lives of the flowers in your arrangements. I learned many of them from experienced florists as an apprentice and discovered a few on my own. I hope they allow you to enjoy the beauty of flowers in your own home for days longer than you've experienced in the past.

Flowers

Always cut flowers with the sharpest knife available and, especially with roses, under water, if possible (in a sink filled with water, submerge the stems and cut them beneath the water's surface).

Never cut stems straight across, always at a steep diagonal. This increases the surface area drawing water into the flowers.

Generally, the shorter you cut the stems, the longer flowers will last.

Hard (or wood)-stem flowers, such as lilacs, roses, hydrangeas — Never smash the ends of the stems as recommended by some florists, because this destroys the structures that transport water up to the flower, thereby preventing water flow. Always cut them with a sharp knife at a diagonal. Adding floral food or, if that's not available, a sugary clear syrup or soda, like Sprite, helps perk them up.

Fruit — Always use wooden skewers (as opposed to metal) to hold fruit together (see arrangements on pages 13 and 32) because the wood soaks up water and expands, holding things together and setting more firmly, especially in floral foam. Always skewer fruit through the core where seed structures will hold it more firmly in place.

Poppies — After you've cut the stems (don't hold them under water to do this and don't cut them at an angle — just straight across) to the desired length, sear the ends with a flame. Strike a match and hold the cut ends of the stems directly in the flame for a few seconds. This helps seal in a milky white substance contained in the stems that keeps them fresh longer.

Bulb Flowers — Replace the water daily to get rid of a slimy substance produced by the stems that uses up oxygen in the water. You can also add a 1/2 teaspoon or so of bleach per half gallon of water to keep the water clean and bacteria-free. Do not put soft-stem, or bulb, flowers in floral foam, only in water.

Hyacinths — Try not to cut off the small bit of bulb left at the end of the stem by most flower sellers; this little bit helps them stay fresh longer.

Tulips — To enliven droopy tulips, wrap them in the florist paper that they were originally wrapped in (or if you didn't save it, newspaper will work), cut the stems at a diagonal, and put them in water, paper and all, for about an hour. They should perk right up.

Materials

Floral foam — Add floral food to the water you're going to soak your floral foam in; do not force the foam under the water—allow it to soak up the water naturally, which may take as long as ten or fifteen minutes. The foam should then soak in the water for an hour or so before inserting the flowers. Allow the flowers you're going to insert into the foam to sit in clean water for at least half an hour before you insert them into the foam.

Floral adhesive — I used floral adhesive (it contains no alcohol) to construct the arrangements on pages 20–21, 36, 71, 74–75, 106–107, 109, and 130. Never use spray adhesive—it will turn flowers and leaves brown.

SOURCE GUIDE

Florists

FLORIST DIRECTORY
www.florist-directory.net
Find your local florist and learn about flowers

Equipment

MICHAELS, THE ARTS AND CRAFTS STORE
Stores nationwide
www.michaels.com
Wide range of florist supplies, vases, and pottery

SMITHERS-OASIS
www.smithersoasis.com
Wide range of florist supplies, such as floral foam,
adhesive, tape, etc.

Home Accessories

NICO DE SWERT
www.nicodeswert.com

TREILLAGE
418 East 75th Street
New York, NY 10021
tel: 212.535.2288
Antique European garden furniture, vases, glassware,
decorative items

ABC CARPET AND HOME
888 Broadway
New York, NY 10003
tel: 212.473.3000
Everything for the home from carpets to furniture to
home accessories, both antique and new

GLOBAL TABLE
107-109 Sullivan Street
New York, NY 10012
tel: 212.431.5839
www.globaltable.com
Tableware from around the world

JAMALI
149 West 28th Street
New York, NY 10001
tel: 212.244.4025
www.jamaligarden.com
Florist tools and equipment, vases, and pottery

CALVIN KLEIN HOME
Stores worldwide
tel: 800.294.7978
Tableware, linens, home accessories

ACKNOWLEDGMENTS

I'd like to extend a huge thank you to Wendell Webber for his indefatigable eye and gorgeous photographs, without which this book would not be; to Jill Groeber for putting it all together so beautifully; to Andrea Danese for working so hard to make it all happen; and especially to Gail Mandel for her wholehearted belief in the project; and to Eric Himmel for his support of my project.

I would also like to thank Tricia Folley and Barbara and Henri Cortes for opening the doors to their beautiful homes.

Special thanks to Sean Scherer for lending his artwork and to everybody at Treillage in New York for making me feel like a kid in a candy store.

My deepest gratitude goes to my good friend and legal advisor, Noah McCay.

And many thanks to those who helped me get to where I am today—I couldn't have done it without you: Ma, Pa, David, Patrick, Monique, Celine, Maurice, Martin, Wilfried, Jules, Jos, Liliane, Els, Ronny, Wim, Anita, Kurt, Philip, Sammy, Dimitri, Cindy, Kizie, Dierdre, Vincent, Pascale, Tom, Jeanine, Daniel, Renny, Eric, KJ, Nicole, Gill, Shanon, Carolina, Nancy, Zina, Ellen, Tom, Rita, Viviane, Mr. Kaas, Mieke, Mark, Chantal, Serge, Amanda, Pierot, Karel, Geert, Dennis, Lars, Martha, Jill, Axel, Marcel, Monique, Pieter, Piet, Gusta, Tage, Brian, Shirin, Sohjo, Fumiko, Pedro, Bert, Mourat, Sabri, Nicolas, Maria, Annie, Jeanine, Peter, Annemarie, Chris, Kris, Nasser, Nader, Momiejoun, Alysia, Eric, Sean, Mark, and Leo.

But most of all, to Nini Ordoubadi for always being there, for pushing me, for believing in me, for inspiring me, for loving me, for saving me . . . thank you.

Editor: Andrea Danese
Designer: Jill Groeber
Production Manager: Justine Keefe

Library of Congress Cataloging-in-Publication Data
De Swert, Nico.
  Living with flowers / by Nico de Swert ; photography by Wendell T. Webber;
  text by Kathleen Hackett.
      p. cm.
  ISBN 10: 0–8109–5895–3
  ISBN 13: 978–0–8109–5895–1
  1. Flower arrangement. I. Webber, Wendell T. II. Hackett, Kathleen. III. Title.

  SB449.D4124 2005
  745.92—dc22
                        2004029348

Published in 2005 by Abrams, an imprint of Harry N. Abrams, Inc.

Printed and bound in China
10 9 8 7 6 5 4 3

harry n. abrams, inc.
a subsidiary of La Martinière Groupe
115 West 18th Street
New York, NY 10011
www.hnabooks.com